Will You?

A Lenten Study
of Baptismal Promises

Cover and interior illustrations by Jason Sierra

Scripture quotations are from the New Revised Standard
Version of the Bible, copyright ©1989 the National Council of
the Churches of Christ in the United States of America.

Psalm quotations are from the Book of Common Prayer.

#2672

ISBN: 978-0-88028-523-0

© 2023 Forward Movement

Forward
Movement
inspire disciples. empower evangelists.

Will You?

A Lenten Study
of Baptismal Promises

Amanda Perkins McGriff

FORWARD MOVEMENT
Cincinnati, Ohio

in collaboration with
Episcopal Evangelism Society

Table of Contents

The Baptismal Covenant

The Book of Common Prayer, pp. 304-305

Celebrant: Do you believe in God the Father?

People: I believe in God, the Father almighty, creator of heaven and earth.

Celebrant: Do you believe in Jesus Christ, the Son of God?

People: I believe in Jesus Christ, his only Son, our Lord. He was conceived by the power of the Holy Spirit and born of the Virgin Mary. He suffered under Pontius Pilate, was crucified, died, and was buried. He descended to the dead. On the third day he rose again. He ascended into heaven, and is seated at the right hand of the Father. He will come again to judge the living and the dead.

Celebrant: Do you believe in God the Holy Spirit?

People: I believe in the Holy Spirit, the holy catholic Church, the communion of saints, the forgiveness of sins, the resurrection of the body, and the life everlasting.

viii

Celebrant: Will you continue in the apostles' teaching and fellowship, in the breaking of the bread, and in the prayers?

People: I will, with God's help.

Celebrant: Will you persevere in resisting evil, and, whenever you fall into sin, repent and return to the Lord?

People: I will, with God's help.

Celebrant: Will you proclaim by word and example the Good News of God in Christ?

People: I will, with God's help.

Celebrant: Will you seek and serve Christ in all persons, loving your neighbor as yourself?

People: I will, with God's help.

Celebrant: Will you strive for justice and peace among all people, and respect the dignity of every human being?

People: I will, with God's help.

Introduction

Holy Baptism is one of the two great sacraments of the gospel given by Christ to his church. Jesus himself was baptized by John at the beginning of his public ministry. The Catechism states that in baptism we are joined with Christ in his death and resurrection, born into God's family, the church, forgiven of our sins, and raised to new life in the Spirit. As part of the service, all who are present renew their own Baptismal Covenant as the newly baptized person is making these promises publicly for the first time. In the case of an infant baptism, sponsors and parents answer on the child's behalf and promise to help the newly baptized live into these promises as they mature. The first three questions of our Baptismal Covenant are about belief, a restatement of our creeds. The last five questions, the "will you" questions, are about action, and these action questions are the focus of this Lenten study. Throughout the season of Lent, we will take a deep look at the promises we make in our baptism using evangelism as our lens.

"Evangelism" is uncomfortable for many Episcopalians, and we'll address the stigma associated both with the word itself and the actions, as well as explore new ways of thinking about evangelism. The "will you" questions of our Baptismal Covenant detail how we are to function within our faith communities and in the wider world as a result of the belief we profess. These "will you" questions follow an arc from a "gathering in" to a "sending out," and this is the arc we will travel together through Lent. These questions are a natural framework for redefining evangelism and laying out a path for living into the promises we make when we answer these questions, "I will, with God's help."

This initiative began as a school project in seminary for a class called "Reimagining Congregations in Mission." The assignment was to design a curriculum outline for a Christian education class specific to my congregational context at the time. After seminary, I received a grant from the Episcopal Evangelism Society to expand on my seminary project and create a five-week daily Lenten curriculum. As the program developed, Forward Movement became a partner as well. This curriculum has been through two piloting phases, and feedback from both phases has been incorporated into the final book and study.

This book has five chapters, each focusing on one of the "will you" questions, and each chapter is divided into seven brief reflections, perfect for daily engagement. These reflections include personal stories, history, theology, and material from common church resources such as scripture, hymns, and liturgy. The closing reflection each week is a brief prayer. If you are participating in this curriculum as part of a small group, this prayer is repeated in the group leader guide as the opening prayer for the group meeting, which ideally would fall on the seventh day of the week's readings. If you are reading this as an individual Lenten discipline, the seventh reflection each week would be best read on Sundays as a part of your worship that day.

Each chapter highlights ministries across the wider church that illustrate the relationship between evangelism and that week's baptismal promise. I have also provided resources and references in an appendix for further exploration. I have intentionally written in a first-person conversational style in part because evangelism is invitational and personal. It is about sharing stories and sharing ourselves and our faith with others. In these reflections, I share my thoughts and theology, shaped by my years in seminary, my work as a hospital chaplain, my vocation as an Episcopal priest, and most importantly, my call as a follower of Christ. These reflections are an opening of the discussion, not an ending to it. Their purpose is to prompt you to reflect on your own experiences and beliefs, and I hope they will prepare you to reframe your understanding of evangelism, either through individual reflection or as part of a lively and fruitful weekly group meeting.

My prayer is that this book will inspire you to think in new ways about the promises we make to God, to each other, and to ourselves in our baptisms.

Thank you for reading and joining in the conversation.

Week One

Will you
continue in
the apostles'
teaching and
fellowship, in
the breaking of
the bread, and
in the prayers?

Will you continue in the apostles' teaching and fellowship, in the breaking of the bread, and in the prayers?

DAY ONE

It may seem counterintuitive to begin a conversation about evangelism with this week's promise. After all, we perceive evangelism as an external action—a going out. And yet this promise seems to draw us inward as we commit to being Christians in community, with God and with each other, all with God's help. But in order to be the church in the world, we must first be the church. Our common life together in a community of faith is the soil in which we grow, providing the nutrients needed to live out the other four "will you" questions.

Before we examine this promise through the lens of evangelism, though, we need to look at the word "evangelism" itself. For many, the word is a stumbling block. When the subject of evangelism is raised, some of us imagine street preachers holding signs threatening damnation and yelling at passing cars. We balk at the idea of initiating what we imagine will be awkward and intrusive conversations or cringe at the thought of exchanging prayers for donations on television. Perhaps you have other experiences you associate with evangelism—some good, some bad. I invite you to pause here and consider your feelings about the word

"evangelism." What images come to mind? Before
moving deeper into the promises we make at baptism, we
must acknowledge these images and stories. Once we've
named them, we can consciously set them aside to make
room for something new.

This study reframes evangelism within the bounds of
the Baptismal Covenant. The commitments we make in
our baptisms offer a guide to the way we are to interact
with the world and the people around us. The newly
baptized promise to be disciples in community with each
other; to repent of sin; to proclaim the Good News; to
look for Christ in all people; and to strive for justice and
peace. Every one of these commitments has something
to say about evangelism, and that is what we will explore
together.

INVITATION

Meditate on the stories and images that come to
mind when you think of the word "evangelism."
Presiding Bishop Michael Curry has called
Episcopalians to a "way of evangelism grounded
in the loving way of Jesus." What does this look
like to you?

Will you continue in the apostles' teaching and fellowship, in the breaking of the bread, and in the prayers?

DAY TWO

Guiding scriptures for this week

Acts 2:42-47
They devoted themselves to the apostles' teaching and fellowship, to the breaking of bread and the prayers. Awe came upon everyone, because many wonders and signs were being done by the apostles. All who believed were together and had all things in common; they would sell their possessions and goods and distribute the proceeds to all, as any had need. Day by day, as they spent much time together in the temple, they broke bread at home and ate their food with glad and generous hearts, praising God and having the goodwill of all the people. And day by day the Lord added to their number those who were being saved.

1 Corinthians 11:23-26
For I received from the Lord what I also handed on to you, that the Lord Jesus on the night when he was betrayed took a loaf of bread, and when he had given thanks, he broke it and said, "This is my body that is for you. Do this in remembrance of me." In the same way he took the cup also, after supper, saying, "This cup is the

new covenant in my blood. Do this, as often as you drink it, in remembrance of me." For as often as you eat this bread and drink the cup, you proclaim the Lord's death until he comes.

1 Corinthians 12:13-27

For in the one Spirit we were all baptized into one body—Jews or Greeks, slaves or free—and we were all made to drink of one Spirit. Indeed, the body does not consist of one member but of many. If the foot would say, "Because I am not a hand, I do not belong to the body," that would not make it any less a part of the body. And if the ear would say, "Because I am not an eye, I do not belong to the body," that would not make it any less a part of the body. If the whole body were an eye, where would the hearing be? If the whole body were hearing, where would the sense of smell be? But as it is, God arranged the members in the body, each one of them, as he chose. If all were a single member, where would the body be? As it is, there are many members, yet one body. The eye cannot say to the hand, "I have no need of you," nor again the head to the feet, "I have no need of you." On the contrary, the members of the body that seem to be weaker are indispensable, and those members of the body that we think less honorable we clothe with greater honor, and our less respectable members are treated with greater respect; whereas our more respectable members do not need this. But God has so arranged the body, giving the greater honor to the inferior member, that there may be no dissension within the body, but the members may have the same care for one another. If one member suffers, all suffer together with it; if one member is honored, all rejoice together with it.

Now you are the body of Christ and individually members of it.

Philippians 4:4-9

Rejoice in the Lord always; again I will say, Rejoice. Let your gentleness be known to everyone. The Lord is near. Do not worry about anything, but in everything by prayer and supplication with thanksgiving let your requests be made known to God. And the peace of God, which surpasses all understanding, will guard your hearts and your minds in Christ Jesus. Finally, beloved, whatever is true, whatever is honorable, whatever is just, whatever is pure, whatever is pleasing, whatever is commendable, if there is any excellence and if there is anything worthy of praise, think about these things. Keep on doing the things that you have learned and received and heard and seen in me, and the God of peace will be with you.

INVITATION

These scriptures have guided the writing of this week's reflections. As you prepare for the remainder of the week, consider what the Bible says about fulfilling this week's baptismal promise. Refer back to these verses throughout the week and make a note of additional scripture references that come to mind as you read.

Will you continue in the apostles' teaching and fellowship, in the breaking of the bread, and in the prayers?

DAY THREE

At seven years old, I walked down the aisle at our small Southern Baptist Church to accept Jesus Christ as my personal Lord and Savior. I was baptized soon afterward. I remember the waders the preacher wore under his robe in the giant baptistery. I remember the handkerchief he held up to the sky before putting it over my nose and mouth to dip me backward into the water. I remember changing quickly into my Sunday clothes and sitting in church with wet hair for the rest of the service. But I do not remember what promises I was asked to make that day.

Whether or not I made the promise to "continue in the apostles' teaching and fellowship, in the breaking of bread, and in the prayers" or something like it, my family took membership in our community of faith seriously. My mother was in the choir. My father taught Sunday School. We ate dinner at church on Wednesdays and breakfast on Sundays. I attended Vacation Bible School, participated in Bible Drill competitions, and was a children's and then youth choir member and an enthusiastic member of our youth group. I was sure these things would always be a part of my life and my children's

lives in much the same way as when I attended Auburn
University and was convinced that my future would
include tailgating at every Auburn home game. Neither
of these dreams survived into adulthood.

I now see some of what I did not see then, such as
how the church of my youth intentionally excluded
some groups of people from full participation in the
congregation's life. But despite these significant concerns,
I remain grateful for the early formation I received as
a part of the Southern Baptist Church, and I miss the
intense commitment to community that was such a part
of my growing up.

INVITATION

If the church was a part of your childhood, consider
how you interacted with your family's congregation.
If you were not involved in church as a child, think
about another intentional community—Little
League, extracurricular activities, etc. What is
different about how you participate in church today,
and what is the same? Were some groups excluded
in those childhood communities? Are they included
now? How have these childhood experiences
shaped your adult life?

Will you continue in the apostles' teaching and fellowship, in the breaking of the bread, and in the prayers?

DAY FOUR

In the book, *This Band of Sisterhood: Black Women Bishops,* edited by Westina Matthews, Bishop Phoebe Roaf is quoted as asking, "Who is not at the table? It may be a Black body or a Brown body, but it also may be a really young body, or it might be a physically challenged body or a transgendered body. At every instance—whether it's been the white church or the Black church or at the diocesan level—somebody's not at the table; and there's so much fear associated with adding a seat or two."

The essence of this first "will you" question is that we cannot be complete or equipped for the work we have been given to do without each other. But if we are looking through an evangelism lens, "each other" cannot just include the people currently in the church pews. It must include people not yet here. This can be complicated. For some, a lifetime of rejection by people of faith means they will need more than a sign declaring that "All are welcome here" to be assured they will not have to fight for their place at the table. If any of God's children are excluded, the body of Christ is diminished, not only in numbers but also in the ability to discern God's call and to see God's vision for the world.

There is no way to make more room at a table without expanding the table or asking those already seated to give up some of the space they are currently occupying. "This-is-the-way-it's-always-been-done-here-like-it-or-leave-it" seems to be more an attitude of assimilation than inclusion. Holding fast what is central to our identity is important, but true welcome means being open to the gifts that the people we encounter will bring to our community, to the lessons they will teach us, and to the ways they will change us.

INVITATION

There is a tension between holding onto who we are as a community and true welcome and inclusion. In what ways has your current church drawn boundaries, for better or worse, around "the way it's always been done here?" In what ways has it made room for new perspectives and growth?

Will you continue in the apostles' teaching and fellowship, in the breaking of the bread, and in the prayers?

DAY FIVE

"Continuing in the prayers" is central to our identity. When most people think about Episcopal prayer, they think about the prayers that form the Book of Common Prayer. This approach makes sense because, as Anglicans, we build community around a communal way of worshipping. Prayers included in the services for eucharist and morning and evening prayer are the foundation of our common life together. The prayer book has hundreds of prayers dealing with all sorts of topics and is an important source for a rich prayer life.

But I believe there is room to expand the table while still honoring our traditions. For instance, there is a growing movement to revive and renew the ancient Christian contemplative tradition. In her book *Centering Prayer and Inner Awakening,* the Rev. Dr. Cynthia Bourgeault makes a case for contemplative prayer "as something that had originally been at the very center of Christian practice and had become lost." She traces the practice of contemplative prayer back to Jesus himself, noting that his "intentional alternation between contemplation and action was fundamental to his way of being in the world."

An example of how this practice is being used to build community can be found at the Center for Spiritual Imagination at the Cathedral of the Incarnation in Garden City, New York. Through a weekly contemplative prayer service and periodic spiritual practice retreats, the congregation models a way to "approach just action as a spiritual practice and a fruit of contemplation."

Another resource for continuing in the prayers is a collection of supplemental liturgical materials called *Enriching Our Worship*. Approved by the wider church in 1997, the collection "is not intended to supplant the Book of Common Prayer, but rather to provide additional resources to assist worshipping communities wishing to expand the language, images, and metaphors used in worship." Please note that the use of these liturgies must be approved by the bishop.

Prayer according to the Book of Common Prayer is a central part of our tradition in the Episcopal Church, but it was never intended to be the only way we pray.

INVITATION

Think about all the different times, places, and ways you pray. How does your prayer practice lead you to respond to the world around you? This week, explore new ways of praying. You might visit the Contemplative Society's website at contemplative.org and click on "Practices." Try one of the contemplative practices listed that you have never tried before. Another possibility is to read through *Enriching Our Worship* and discuss whether there's a liturgy or set of prayers you'd like your church to consider. Some samples of the liturgies are available online.

To learn more about the Cathedral of the Incarnation Garden City's Center for Spiritual Imagination, visit spiritualimagination.org.

DAY SIX

Will you continue in the apostles' teaching and fellowship, in the breaking of bread, and in the prayers?

In the eucharist, we combine our promises to continue in the breaking of bread and in the prayers. At the end of every eucharistic service, we say a post-communion prayer together. In this prayer, we thank God for nourishing us with the eucharistic meal and ask God to send us into the world in ministry. This prayer acknowledges that the bread and wine we have just shared in communion are nourishment for participating in God's work in the world.

Post-communion Prayers
The Book of Common Prayer, pp. 365-366

Eternal God, heavenly Father,
you have graciously accepted us as living members
of your Son our Savior Jesus Christ,
and you have fed us with spiritual food
in the Sacrament of his Body and Blood.
Send us now into the world in peace,
and grant us strength and courage
to love and serve you
with gladness and singleness of heart;
through Christ our Lord. *Amen.*

or the following

Almighty and everliving God,
we thank you for feeding us with the spiritual food
of the most precious Body and Blood
of your Son our Savior Jesus Christ;
and for assuring us in these holy mysteries
that we are living members of the Body of your Son,
and heirs of your eternal kingdom.
And now, Father, send us out
to do the work you have given us to do,
to love and serve you
as faithful witnesses of Christ our Lord.
To him, to you, and to the Holy Spirit,
be honor and glory, now and for ever. *Amen.*

INVITATION

Choose one of the post-communion prayers
included in today's reflection and use it to
meditate on the work you have been given to
do. How does the eucharist nourish and form
you for your ministry?

DAY SEVEN

Will you continue in the apostles' teaching and fellowship, in the breaking of bread, and in the prayers?

Prayer for the Unity of the Church
The Book of Common Prayer, p. 818

O God the Father of our Lord Jesus Christ, our only Savior, the Prince of Peace: Give us grace seriously to lay to heart the great dangers we are in by our unhappy divisions; take away all hatred and prejudice, and whatever else may hinder us from godly union and concord; that, as there is but one Body and one Spirit, one hope of our calling, one Lord, one Faith, one Baptism, one God and Father of us all, so we may be all of one heart and of one soul, united in one holy bond of truth and peace, of faith and charity, and may with one mind and one mouth glorify thee; through Jesus Christ our Lord. *Amen.*

Week Two

Will you
persevere in
resisting evil,
and, whenever
you fall into
sin, repent and
return to the
Lord?

Will you persevere in resisting evil, and, whenever you fall into sin, repent and return to the Lord?

DAY ONE

This week, we will focus on sin. If you thought evangelism had some baggage, the implications of this word are enough for a whole steamer trunk. Many of us likely have an uncomfortable relationship with the word. Maybe it gives us flashbacks of a church community that sought to shame followers onto a path of righteousness. Perhaps we're leery of a word that has been used to categorize and sometimes demean others. We're shellshocked by platitudes such as "love the sinner, hate the sin," and we reel from communities that have decided that the way to "save the sinful" is through fear, condemnation, and punishment.

But just as love is the way of Jesus, so too is repentance from sin a part of the life of faith. Followers of Jesus seek to mold ourselves day by day, decision by decision, into the likeness of Christ so that we, like Christ, can communicate God's love to the world. When we fail to do that—in what we do and what we have left undone—we sin. But sin is not the final stop on this journey of faith. This week's "will you" question provides the possibility of repentance for sin. Instead of being a path of fear and condemnation and punishment, followers of Jesus travel a path of awe and compassion and liberation. Along this way, we acknowledge what we have done and repent for it, when necessary, not because we are frightened into doing so or so that we can shroud ourselves in shame and guilt, but so we can become more and more who we were created to be. This is a way of love that leads us to *life* in Christ.

If you find the prospect of a week focused on sin unsettling, I would say that you are not alone. I do, too. But I hope you will be open to that disturbance and use this week to examine your thinking about sin, repentance, and return. Consider what these loaded words mean for you individually and for the church corporately and how the definitions we apply to them affect our ability to proclaim the Good News of God's love for all people, including ourselves.

INVITATION

Has a faith group's theology of sin and repentance been harmful to you or someone you love in the past? Reflect on that experience. What do you consider to be a sin? What does repentance mean to you?

Will you persevere in resisting evil, and, whenever you fall into sin, repent and return to the Lord?

DAY TWO

Guiding scriptures for this week

Genesis 1:26-27
Then God said, "Let us make humankind in our image, according to our likeness; and let them have dominion over the fish of the sea, and over the birds of the air, and over the cattle, and over all the wild animals of the earth, and over every creeping thing that creeps upon the earth." So God created humankind in his image, in the image of God he created them; male and female he created them.

Psalm 51:11-20
Create in me a clean heart, O God;
    and renew a right spirit within me.
Cast me not away from your presence
    and take not your holy Spirit from me.
Give me the joy of your saving help again
    and sustain me with your bountiful Spirit.
I shall teach your ways to the wicked,
    and sinners shall return to you.
Deliver me from death, O God,
    and my tongue shall sing of your righteousness,
    O God of my salvation.

Open my lips, O Lord,
    and my mouth shall proclaim your praise.
Had you desired it, I would have offered sacrifice,
    but you take no delight in burnt-offerings.
The sacrifice of God is a troubled spirit;
    a broken and contrite heart, O God,
        you will not despise.
Be favorable and gracious to Zion,
    and rebuild the walls of Jerusalem.
Then you will be pleased with the appointed sacrifices,
with burnt-offerings and oblations;
    then shall they offer young bullocks upon your altar.

Matthew 7:12-14
In everything do to others as you would have them do to you; for this is the law and the prophets. Enter through the narrow gate; for the gate is wide and the road is easy that leads to destruction, and there are many who take it. For the gate is narrow and the road is hard that leads to life, and there are few who find it.

1 John 1:5-10
This is the message we have heard from him and proclaim to you, that God is light and in him there is no darkness at all. If we say that we have fellowship with him while we are walking in darkness, we lie and do not do what is true; but if we walk in the light as he himself is in the light, we have fellowship with one another, and the blood of Jesus his Son cleanses us from all sin.

If we say that we have no sin, we deceive ourselves, and the truth is not in us. If we confess our sins, he who is faithful and just will forgive us our sins and cleanse us from all unrighteousness. If we say that we have not sinned, we make him a liar, and his word is not in us.

INVITATION

As you prepare for the remainder of this week, consider what the Bible has to say about fulfilling this week's baptismal promise. Refer back to these verses throughout the week, and make note of additional scripture references that come to mind as you read.

DAY THREE

Will you persevere in resisting evil, and, whenever you fall into sin, repent and return to the Lord?

In the Ash Wednesday Liturgy from the Book of Common Prayer, all are invited, "in the name of the Church, to the observance of a holy Lent, by self-examination and repentance; by prayer, fasting, and self-denial; and by reading and meditation on God's holy Word" (p. 265). We have been given this season of Lent to focus our attention on self-examination so that we can more clearly see the truth that is in us.

In her *Revelations of Divine Love*, 14th-century mystic Julian of Norwich wrote that our souls are grounded in God, for everyone, everywhere, all the time because this grounding in God is what it means to be human. She believed that sin does not break our connection with God, but it can cause us to view our connection with God as broken. Author Ellyn Sanna offers in her book, *All Shall Be Well: A Modern-Language Version of the Revelation of Julian of Norwich,* an interpretation of Julian's Sixteenth Revelation: "I cried because our spiritual eyes are so blind, and we are so weighed down by our mortal flesh and the darkness of sin that we cannot see clearly... And because our eyes are so dim, we can scarcely believe or trust in God's great love and our own utter safety." So our work toward repentance and reconciliation and healing does not draw us closer to God because that is impossible. It allows us to accept the reality that we have never been outside of God's embrace.

Acknowledging our sinfulness is not about self-flagellation and mortification. It is about clearing away the distortions that sin creates so that we can see and treat ourselves and others as beloved children of God, created in God's image.

INVITATION

I invite you to reflect on and respond to another of Julian's teachings on sin: "When we look at another who has fallen into sin, we should focus only on compassion and our own brokenness, longing for God's healing for us both. Without this attitude, our own souls will trip and stumble into sin. Compassion is our protection."

DAY FOUR

Will you persevere in resisting evil, and, whenever you fall into sin, repent and return to the Lord?

"Any doubts you have will soon disappear." Years ago, I received this message from the beyond via fortune cookie, and I still carry it in my wallet because it was so unsettling to me at the time. Perhaps I take fortune cookies a little too seriously, but my strong negative reaction to this particular fortune crystallized for me how important doubt is to my faith.

If I never question my path, if I am always certain that I have it all figured out, then I don't leave room for direction or redirection from the Holy Spirit. I want to continue wrestling with God and myself, to doubt that I am fully living into who I was created to be. And I want that same spirit of self-examination for the church. What kind of redirection is possible for the church if we, its members, never question its actions or inaction?

From the late 1800s to the mid-1900s, the federal government operated Native American boarding schools in partnership with Christian denominations, including the Episcopal Church. In order to forcefully assimilate Indigenous children into Euro-American culture, the children were separated from their families and raised in residential schools where they were prevented from speaking their Native languages, wearing traditional dress, and practicing their religions. It was only in 2022, more than 50 years after the end of the boarding school program, that the Episcopal Church officially committed to "the work of truth-telling and reconciliation around its role in Indigenous residential boarding schools."

This is one example of many corporate sins from the church's past. Where are the places in our church today of blindness to evil, silence about it, or even participation in it? Discovering the answers to these questions and setting ourselves on a path to repentance and reconciliation begins with doubt.

INVITATION

The Episcopal Church, through a General Convention Resolution, encourages dioceses to conduct an audit "of all Indigenous peoples whose ancestral and territorial homelands its churches and buildings now occupy." What is the history of Indigenous peoples in your area? What does, or could, your parish do to acknowledge and respond to its place in that history and its use of Native lands?

DAY FIVE

*Will you persevere in
resisting evil, and,
whenever you fall into sin,
repent and return to the Lord?*

Confession of Sin
The Book of Common Prayer, p. 352

Most merciful God,
we confess that we have sinned against you
in thought, word, and deed,
by what we have done,
and by what we have left undone.
We have not loved you with our whole heart;
we have not loved our neighbors as ourselves.
We are truly sorry and we humbly repent.
For the sake of your Son Jesus Christ,
have mercy on us and forgive us;
that we may delight in your will,
and walk in your ways,
to the glory of your Name. *Amen.*

INVITATION

Spend time with the words of this familiar
confession, examining each phrase
individually for the ways in which our sin
causes us to see ourselves and others as
separated from God. In *Enriching
Our Worship,* the confession offers this
language instead: "We repent of the
evil that enslaves us, the evil we have
done, and the evil done on our
behalf." What do you think is meant
by "the evil that enslaves us" and
"the evil done on our behalf?" Why
would we need to repent for the evil
someone else has done?

DAY SIX

Will you persevere in resisting evil, and, whenever you fall into sin, repent and return to the Lord?

When we think of evangelism, we usually think of work with people outside our church doors. But this week's "will you" question leads us to the truth that evangelism work must begin with ourselves, with attempting to untangle the web of deceptions that prevent us from seeing and treating ourselves and others as created in God's own image.

To that end, Jen Holt Enriquez and Will Bouvel from the Diocese of Chicago developed a children's curriculum called *Tell Me the Truth About Racism*. It started with a book that they wrote together, *The Big Lie of Racism*, and has expanded into a Lenten children's program. They received a Becoming Beloved Community grant to expand training for those interested in bringing this teaching into their congregations. Their approach defines racism as "'the lie in our world that some people are better than others based on the color of their skin.' It is only because of the Truth we know from God, that all people are equally children of God, that we can clearly define racism as a lie."

One of the truths we must acknowledge about ourselves is that the Anglican Communion's worldwide reach is, at least in part, a result of centuries of partnerships with colonial power and white supremacy disguised as evangelism. This is another reason that the word evangelism is uncomfortable for us. For more information about the church's historic entanglements with power structures and profit-seeking, I recommend joining a "Sacred Ground" dialogue circle. In this program, "participants are invited to peel away the layers that have contributed to the challenges and divides of the present day—all while grounded in our call to faith, hope and love." I am proud to be part of a church actively engaging in the difficult work of acknowledging the truth of our sinfulness and trying to make amends for it.

INVITATION

I invite you to visit the Sacred Ground website at episcopalchurch.org/sacred-ground/ to read "A Message from the Rev. Canon Stephanie Spellers," specifically thinking about how the four quadrants of the spiritual path connect to the last four "will you" questions of the Baptismal Covenant.

To learn more about *Tell Me the Truth About Racism*, visit tellmethetruthaboutracism.org.

DAY SEVEN

*Will you persevere in
resisting evil, and,
whenever you fall into sin,
repent and return to the Lord?*

Prayer for the Church
The Book of Common Prayer, p. 816

Gracious Father, we pray for thy holy catholic Church.
Fill it with all truth, in all truth with all peace. Where it
is corrupt, purify it; where it is in error, direct it; where
in any thing it is amiss, reform it. Where it is right,
strengthen it; where it is in want, provide for it; where it
is divided, reunite it; for the sake of Jesus Christ thy Son
our Savior. *Amen.*

Week Three

Will you
proclaim by
word and
example the
Good News
of God in
Christ?

*Will you proclaim by word
and example the Good News
of God in Christ?*

DAY ONE

With this week's "will you" question, we move from an
inward focus on forming community and acknowledging
and repenting for our sins to looking outside ourselves
and proclaiming the Good News to others. The work
of our first two baptismal promises is an essential
foundation for this week because we must first be
transformed by the Good News of God in Christ before
we can share it with others.

We need to be able to articulate our own stories of how
we have been transformed by the overwhelming love
and mercy of God, as revealed in the life, death, and
resurrection of Jesus Christ. This requires reflection on
where we have seen the hand of God at work in our own
lives, in big moments and small, in times of celebration
and crisis, in the everyday and the extraordinary. To
share our stories, we need to know them.

Another important piece of living into this baptismal
promise is the invitation to hear others proclaim by word
and example the Good News. Sharing is a mutual act.
Jesus invited people's stories, and he listened deeply. We
are called to do the same.

Sharing our faith can be scary. It can expose insecurities and vulnerabilities that can make it tempting to revert to judgment and arrogance. For example, it is much easier to focus on how someone else needs to change than on how we have been changed ourselves. And it is more comfortable to tell someone about what we know rather than about what we have experienced. In her book, *Walking on Water: Reflections on Faith and Art*, Madeleine L'Engle writes, "We do not draw people to Christ by loudly discrediting what they believe, by telling them how wrong they are and how right we are, but by showing them a light that is so lovely that they want with all their hearts to know the source of it."

INVITATION

Read the Evangelism Charter for the Episcopal Church, found at episcopalchurch.org/ministries/evangelism/toolkit/foundations. Reflect on your story of "encounter, Good News, and resurrection in Jesus."

*Will you proclaim by word
and example the Good News
of God in Christ?*

DAY TWO

Guiding scriptures for this week

Matthew 5:13-16

You are the salt of the earth; but if salt has lost its taste,
how can its saltiness be restored? It is no longer good for
anything, but is thrown out and trampled under foot.
You are the light of the world. A city built on a hill cannot
be hidden. No one after lighting a lamp puts it under the
bushel basket, but on the lampstand, and it gives light
to all in the house. In the same way, let your light shine
before others, so that they may see your good works and
give glory to your Father in heaven.

Luke 19:1-10

He entered Jericho and was passing through it. A man
was there named Zacchaeus; he was a chief tax collector
and was rich. He was trying to see who Jesus was, but on
account of the crowd he could not, because he was short
in stature. So he ran ahead and climbed a sycamore tree
to see him, because he was going to pass that way. When
Jesus came to the place, he looked up and said to him,
"Zacchaeus, hurry and come down; for I must stay at
your house today." So he hurried down and was happy

to welcome him. All who saw it began to grumble and said, "He has gone to be the guest of one who is a sinner." Zacchaeus stood there and said to the Lord, "Look, half of my possessions, Lord, I will give to the poor; and if I have defrauded anyone of anything, I will pay back four times as much." Then Jesus said to him, "Today salvation has come to this house, because he too is a son of Abraham. For the Son of Man came to seek out and to save the lost."

Romans 12:9-17

Let love be genuine; hate what is evil, hold fast to what is good; love one another with mutual affection; outdo one another in showing honor. Do not lag in zeal, be ardent in spirit, serve the Lord. Rejoice in hope, be patient in suffering, persevere in prayer. Contribute to the needs of the saints; extend hospitality to strangers. Bless those who persecute you; bless and do not curse them. Rejoice with those who rejoice, weep with those who weep. Live in harmony with one another; do not be haughty, but associate with the lowly; do not claim to be wiser than you are. Do not repay anyone evil for evil, but take thought for what is noble in the sight of all.

INVITATION

As you prepare for the remainder of the week, consider what the Bible has to say about fulfilling this week's baptismal promise. Refer back to these verses throughout the week and make note of additional scripture references that come to mind as you read.

DAY THREE

*Will you proclaim by word
and example the Good News
of God in Christ?*

At the church camp of my youth, we made witnessing
bracelets that had different colored beads for the
individual parts of the plan of salvation. Black represented
sin. Red was for the blood of Jesus that cleansed us from
sin and led to the white bead, symbolizing forgiveness.
Blue was for the water of a believer's baptism, green for
continued growth in faith, and yellow for heaven, our
eternal reward. After making the bracelet, we memorized
a Bible verse associated with each bead and practiced
"sharing our faith" with each other.

The idea was that we would wear our bracelets out in
the world, and people would ask us about them, giving
us spontaneous opportunities to witness. I grew up in
Montgomery, Alabama, and there were a lot of these
bracelets around, so most people I came into contact
with were already familiar with them. Besides that, I was
a quiet, shy, and sheltered kid who didn't exactly invite
questions from strangers. So, all my practice and crafting
went unused. This reflection is the first time I have
actually communicated with anyone about a witnessing
bracelet outside of those long-ago summer camp
rehearsals.

As an adult, I think very differently about what it means
to proclaim the Good News. Now, sharing my faith
is about conversation, connection, and relationship.
It is about shared stories and experiences, caring and
compassion for those who are hurting, and rejoicing
with those who are celebrating. I don't have to wait for
someone else to ask just the right question. I simply have
to see and be fully present to the people I encounter and
to the leading of the Holy Spirit. It's not as clear-cut as
back in that youth group: there's no established script or
prescribed visual aids. But I never lack occasions to share
my faith. Opportunities abound.

INVITATION

How has your definition
of "proclaiming the
Good News" changed
over time? How do you
share your faith in your
daily life? What have
been the results of
your efforts?

DAY FOUR

*Will you proclaim by word
and example the Good News
of God in Christ?*

There's a Wideness in God's Mercy

There's a wideness in God's mercy
like the wideness of the sea;
there's a kindness in his justice,
which is more than liberty.
There is welcome for the sinner,
and more graces for the good;
there is mercy with the Savior;
there is healing in his blood.

There is no place where earth's sorrows
are more felt than up in heaven;
there is no place where earth's failings
have such kindly judgment given.
There is plentiful redemption
in the blood that has been shed;
there is joy for all the members
in the sorrows of the Head.

For the love of God is broader
than the measure of the mind;
and the heart of the Eternal
is most wonderfully kind.
If our love were but more faithful,
we should take him at his word;
and our life would be thanksgiving
for the goodness of the Lord.

Lyrics by Frederick William Faber,
The Hymnal 1982, 469

INVITATION

Which hymns, scriptures, poetry, liturgy, or
visual artworks have shaped your thoughts
and feelings about the
Good News? Art itself
can be invitational. How
does, or could, your
church open the door to
relationship with your
community through
shared experiences of
art and beauty?

DAY FIVE

*Will you proclaim by word
and example the Good News
of God in Christ?*

"Radical hospitality" is a phrase that we like to use a lot
in the Episcopal Church. What we usually mean is that
all people are welcome to come and be a part of our
churches. But in a relationship, hospitality is given and
received by both parties. Jesus had a habit of turning
hospitality on its head throughout his ministry. The
hospitality that Jesus offered in the gospel stories is
unique in that he often invited those more marginalized
than himself to host him.

I am a hospital chaplain, and one reason my job exists is
because people can feel extreme dislocation in hospitals.
By that, I mean their normal connections to identity,
place, and experience seem to be stripped away. They are
outside of their normal routines and sources of support,
clad in uncomfortable (and revealing) clothing, and
poked and prodded at all hours of the day and night.
Patients are often frightened and confused by what is
going on. My job is, in part, to be hospitable: to help
orient patients to the hospital environment and available
resources, to accompany them through the strangeness of
illness and loss and trauma, and to help them connect to
their sources of meaning and hope.

But my job is also to receive hospitality. I continue to be amazed at and honored by the depth of hospitality offered by those who invite me into their experience, particularly during a time of disorientation and loss. It is one thing to extend hospitality from a place of order and familiarity. It is another thing entirely to welcome a stranger into a house that's a wreck, where the kids are screaming and dinner is burned and cold.

We like to look put together, like we have all the answers and are completely self-sufficient. But relationship is deepened when we abandon the notion that we have to appear at our best in order to attract and keep the attention of the other. Relationship is strengthened when we share stories of issues not yet resolved and ongoing transformation. Relationship happens when we truly invite people into our hopes and fears and joys and sorrows.

INVITATION

Consider how you practice hospitality in your own life and how you accept the hospitality of others. How open are you to reaching out and asking for help and guidance in a time of need or confusion? How open is your church to doing the same?

DAY SIX

*Will you proclaim by word
and example the Good News
of God in Christ?*

The community of St. Paul's Episcopal Church in Richmond, Virginia, is actively welcoming people into its vulnerability. This parish was once known as "the Cathedral of the Confederacy" because of its ties to Confederate leaders like Jefferson Davis and Robert E. Lee and its pro-slavery stance and theology during the Confederate era. In 2015, in response to the racially motivated murder of nine African Americans during Bible study at the Emanuel African Methodist Episcopal Church in Charleston, South Carolina, the vestry of St. Paul's authorized the formation of the History and Reconciliation Initiative. This group was charged with acknowledging and making amends for the church's racial history.

They began by removing the many Confederate symbols and plaques within the church and, over the following years, moved on to acknowledging the full truth of their own history. They continue this work by seeking opportunities to participate in redemption and reconciliation between races in their community. They are listening and learning as they go.

St. Paul's website explains: "We are part of a living and evolving history—a journey toward becoming a beloved community in service to racial healing and justice. While our church is rooted in great injustice, our story reveals great transformation and courage among our members... Taken together, our whole story provokes us to think about repentance. To repent is to turn around. We are turning. There is turning yet to do."

The first step in proclaiming the Good News is realizing how God's love and mercy have transformed us—and how they are transforming us still—from who we thought we were to who we were created to be. St. Paul's is continuing to turn, changing not only its own story going forward but also impacting its community through its reconciling action.

INVITATION

Discernment about changes to the images and symbols in our worship spaces is complex and controversial. Think about your worship space. What does it proclaim about your history, what you value, who is welcome, and how you see God?

To learn more about the History and Reconciliation Initiative at St. Paul's Richmond, visit stpaulsrva.org/HRI.

*Will you proclaim by word
and example the Good News
of God in Christ?*

DAY SEVEN

The General Thanksgiving
The Book of Common Prayer, p. 101

Almighty God, Father of all mercies,
we your unworthy servants give you humble thanks
for all your goodness and loving-kindness
to us and to all whom you have made.
We bless you for our creation, preservation,
and all the blessings of this life;
but above all for your immeasurable love
in the redemption of the world by our Lord Jesus Christ;
for the means of grace, and for the hope of glory.
And, we pray, give us such an awareness of your mercies,
that with truly thankful hearts we may show forth
        your praise,
not only with our lips, but in our lives,
by giving up our selves to your service,
and by walking before you
in holiness and righteousness all our days;
through Jesus Christ our Lord,
to whom, with you and the Holy Spirit,
be honor and glory throughout all ages. *Amen.*

Week Four

Will you seek
and serve Christ
in all persons,
loving your
neighbor as
yourself?

Will you seek and serve Christ in all persons, loving your neighbor as yourself?

DAY ONE

As Christians, we are to work to reconcile all people to God and to each other. In his book *Tattoos on the Heart: The Power of Boundless Compassion*, Jesuit priest Fr. Greg Boyle writes, "We imagine, with God, this circle of compassion. Then we imagine no one standing outside of that circle." This is the essence of this week's "will you" question. We each have our own circle of compassion, and we make decisions, conscious and unconscious, about who is allowed inside our circle and who remains on the outside.

This week's question calls us to go to the boundaries of our circles, to the lines that this world and our culture have drawn, to the walls we have built to separate ourselves from one another and to push outward. We are to receive all people as the beloved children of God that they are, and we are to ask to be received in return.

We are all made in the image of God and grounded in the love of God. But there is an idea that's taken root in the world that a person's worth can be determined by race, economic status, ability, belief system, sexuality, or behavior. I do not believe this is God's vision of the world. This is a vision of the world created by the world, and it is a sign of the world's brokenness and sinfulness.

We must push back against these pervasive delusions and seek to dismantle the barriers that exclude. We go to our margins to ask those we find there to teach us how to be a neighbor to them and how to see Christ in them. Through this learning, we can see a clearer image of Christ within ourselves. As Boyle writes, "We imagine, with God," a world free from margins. Let us go to our margins and work to erase them.

INVITATION

"Compassion" has become a loaded word, co-opted by advertisers, politicians, and sappy movies. What is your definition of compassion? Who resides at the margins of your circle of compassion? What would it mean to ask to be received by those on the margins and to seek to learn from them instead of trying to help them?

*Will you seek and serve
Christ in all persons, loving
your neighbor as yourself?*

Guiding scriptures for this week

Psalm 139:12-16

For you yourself created my inmost parts;
    you knit me together in my mother's womb.
I will thank you because I am marvelously made;
    your works are wonderful, and I know it well.
My body was not hidden from you,
    while I was being made in secret
    and woven in the depths of the earth.
Your eyes beheld my limbs, yet unfinished in the womb;
all of them were written in your book;
    they were fashioned day by day,
    when as yet there was none of them.
How deep I find your thoughts, O God!
    how great is the sum of them!

Luke 10:25-37

Just then a lawyer stood up to test Jesus. "Teacher," he
said, "what must I do to inherit eternal life?" He said
to him, "What is written in the law? What do you read
there?" He answered, "You shall love the Lord your God
with all your heart, and with all your soul, and with all

your strength, and with all your mind; and your neighbor as yourself." And he said to him, "You have given the right answer; do this, and you will live." But wanting to justify himself, he asked Jesus, "And who is my neighbor?" Jesus replied, "A man was going down from Jerusalem to Jericho, and fell into the hands of robbers, who stripped him, beat him, and went away, leaving him half dead. Now by chance a priest was going down that road; and when he saw him, he passed by on the other side. So likewise a Levite, when he came to the place and saw him, passed by on the other side. But a Samaritan while traveling came near him; and when he saw him, he was moved with pity. He went to him and bandaged his wounds, having poured oil and wine on them. Then he put him on his own animal, brought him to an inn, and took care of him. The next day he took out two denarii, gave them to the innkeeper, and said, 'Take care of him; and when I come back, I will repay you whatever more you spend.' Which of these three, do you think, was a neighbor to the man who fell into the hands of the robbers?" He said, "The one who showed him mercy." Jesus said to him, "Go and do likewise."

2 Corinthians 5:14-21

For the love of Christ urges us on, because we are convinced that one has died for all; therefore all have died. And he died for all, so that those who live might live no longer for themselves, but for him who died and was raised for them.

From now on, therefore, we regard no one from a human point of view; even though we once knew Christ from a human point of view, we know him no longer in that way. So if anyone is in Christ, there is a new creation: everything old has passed away; see, everything has become new! All this is from God, who reconciled us to himself through Christ, and has given us the ministry of reconciliation; that is, in Christ God was reconciling the world to himself, not counting their trespasses against them, and entrusting the message of reconciliation to us. So we are ambassadors for Christ, since God is making his appeal through us; we entreat you on behalf of Christ, be reconciled to God. For our sake he made him to be sin who knew no sin, so that in him we might become the righteousness of God.

INVITATION

As you prepare for the remainder of the week, consider what the Bible says about fulfilling this week's baptismal promise. Refer back to these verses throughout the week and make a note of additional scripture references that come to mind as you read.

DAY THREE

*Will you seek and serve
Christ in all persons, loving
your neighbor as yourself?*

My grandmother died from early-onset Alzheimer's at
age 63, and since then, the people affected by this disease
have had a special place in my heart. I was 12 years old
when my grandmother died, and I was not allowed to
see her for a time before she died because my parents
did not want me to remember her as she was in the final
months of her disease. When I was part of the pastoral
care staff at my sending parish before I entered seminary,
I worked with some of our parishioners who had
advanced Alzheimer's. It was a healing and life-giving
experience for me.

The Founders Place Ministry at St. Luke's Episcopal
Church in Birmingham, Alabama, "seeks to end the
isolation of dementia" through a program that provides
both respite for caregivers and safe and engaging
fellowship opportunities for those with memory loss.
They also offer a caregiver support group and training for
volunteers on how to make meaningful connections with
someone living with dementia. Their website explains:
"Through visual art, movement, music, storytelling,
games, and fellowship, Founders Place respite program
stimulates cognition, nurtures growth, and provides

purpose and meaning for participants with memory loss, as well as dedicated volunteers who serve as intentional companions."

Many times, those in advanced stages of Alzheimer's or dementia must go to a residential care facility, and continued relationship with the church community relies on personal visits. But it can be difficult to understand how a visit with someone in the final stages of Alzheimer's can be meaningful. These visits are not easy, and the truth is that it is often impossible to tell whether the person being visited is even aware someone else is in the room. However, I have been present when a lifelong Episcopalian who was seemingly non-communicative very clearly said "daily bread" at the appropriate point in the Lord's Prayer. I have seen people briefly come out of the fog of this disease to enjoy an old hymn. These moments are clear indications to me that being remembered and cared for as part of the body of Christ is deeply meaningful, even when that meaning can no longer be communicated in traditional ways.

INVITATION

What other groups are frequently overlooked
in conversations about inclusion
and full participation in the
life of the church because
of intellectual and
physical differences?
How does, or could,
your church welcome members of these groups
while treating them as individuals?

To learn more about the Founders Place
ministry at St. Luke's Birmingham, visit
saint-lukes.com/ministries/founders-place.

Will you seek and serve Christ in all persons, loving your neighbor as yourself?

DAY FOUR

When I hear the phrase, "Love your neighbor as yourself," the first story that comes to mind is the parable of the good Samaritan. Jesus shows us through this parable that God's definition of "neighbor" differs from society's. Being a neighbor is dependent on our actions, not our social location. A neighbor shows mercy, even to someone society would consider untouchable or "other."

I don't think it's an accident that Jesus would have been "other" to most of us. God did not become incarnate as a ruler or member of a privileged class. God became incarnate in a first-century Jew, part of a community with a long history of pain and suffering that included defeat, exile, and enslavement. As an infant, Jesus and his parents became refugees in the land of Egypt, fleeing a despotic and insecure ruler under cover of night. His earthly father was not a high priest or an important official in the Jewish community. He was a carpenter, a trade in which Jesus himself was most likely trained.

As an adult, Jesus drew large crowds, but this did not change the fact that he was an itinerant rabbi, apparently homeless, relying on the provision of God through the kindness of strangers and patronage of followers. The Rev. Dr. Kelly Brown Douglas, in her book *Stand Your Ground: Black Bodies and the Justice of God*, points out that "on the cross, Jesus fully divests himself of all pretensions to power, privilege, and exceptionalism, even as the incarnate revelation of God... Jesus's identification with the lynched/crucified class is not accidental. It is intentional. It did not begin with his death on the cross. In fact, that Jesus was crucified signals his prior bond with the 'crucified class' of his day." It also signals his bond with the persecuted and marginalized of this and every time.

INVITATION

Which group in your community most resembles the persecuted and marginalized status of first-century Jews in the Roman Empire? How does, or could, your church actively seek and serve Christ in the members of this group?

Will you seek and serve Christ in all persons, loving your neighbor as yourself?

DAY FIVE

A challenging part of my job as a hospital chaplain is to change the power dynamic that naturally exists when a caregiver walks into a patient's room. Caregiving is a powerful position because one person in the relationship is the giver of care, and the other is the recipient.

But I don't see myself as the one with the power, and I try to convey that in many different ways in my interactions. Some ways are physical. During my work, I wear clothes with enough pockets so that I can carry around my patient lists without needing a clipboard or something else official-looking in my hands. When an extra chair is not available, I do a lot of squatting at bedsides and beside chairs so that I can be at or below eye level with a patient or family member who has something they'd like to talk about instead of standing over them.

And some ways I try to lessen the power differential involve my approach to chaplaincy. My job isn't to bring God into patients' rooms. I have no need or ability to cart God from room to room. Instead, I am meeting the God who is already there, trying to understand the way that patients are experiencing God's movement and healing for themselves. This approach allows me to enter with a sense of wonder and curiosity, to see each patient as someone who can teach me not only about themselves and their needs but also about God.

It is too easy to limit God, to stuff God into a box of our own making, if we only look for God in the echo chambers that many of our churches have become. Encounters with the stranger open our imaginations, helping us see and experience God in new ways, adding depth, layers, and fresh perspectives to our faith. This is the true gift of caring for the stranger both in the hospital and in the wider world.

INVITATION

In what ways do you interact with people who believe or worship differently than you do? How is your faith threatened and how is it strengthened by these interactions? What does, or could, your church do to promote interfaith or interdenominational dialogue and cooperation?

Will you seek and serve Christ in all persons, loving your neighbor as yourself?

DAY SIX

On Maundy Thursday each year, we commemorate Jesus's final meal with his disciples prior to his crucifixion, when he gave us a new commandment: "Love one another. Just as I have loved you, you also should love one another. By this everyone will know that you are my disciples, if you have love for one another." (John 13:34b-35).

Jesus knew that his hour had come. He was about to be betrayed, arrested, tried, and murdered. He had one last opportunity to help the disciples understand his message. They had followed him, listened to him teach, and watched him heal. They had heard all the parables. And they still, pretty clearly, didn't get it. He knew that in the days to come, there would be times of fear, testing, and failure for his disciples. The crucifixion was the day Jesus proclaimed God's love for the world. But the Last Supper was when he showed his followers that he loved them individually and personally, when he taught us how to share this love with others. He did this by touching their dry, cracked, and dirty feet. He held their feet in his own hands, one at a time, and he cleansed them.

In this season of Lent, as we prepare for the drama and ritual of Holy Week and the pageantry and celebration of resurrection at Easter, let us not lose sight of the way to which we are being called. Let us constantly go to the margins of our own circles, not to change the people we find there, but to allow them to change us. Let our hearts be ever-expanding and our circles of inclusion be ever-widening. Let us not be defined by our traditions but by our love.

INVITATION

So many in our communities are going through times of fear, testing, and failure. I invite you to think about ways you and your faith community can demonstrate God's love and care for them by meeting basic needs, like cleanliness and comfort, in a manner that respects their dignity.

Will you seek and serve Christ in all persons, loving your neighbor as yourself?

DAY SEVEN

Maundy Thursday Liturgy
The Book of Common Prayer, pp. 274-275

The Lord Jesus, after he had supped with his disciples and had washed their feet, said to them, "Do you know what I, your Lord and Master, have done to you? I have given you an example, that you should do as I have done."

Peace is my last gift to you, my own peace I now leave with you; peace which the world cannot give, I give to you.

I give you a new commandment: Love one another as I have loved you.

Peace is my last gift to you, my own peace I now leave with you; peace which the world cannot give, I give to you.

By this shall the world know that you are my disciples: That you have love for one another.

Week Five

Will you strive
for justice and
peace among
all people,
and respect
the dignity of
every human
being?

Will you strive for justice and peace among all people, and respect the dignity of every human being?

DAY ONE

Our final week's "will you" question is about justice, peace, respect, and dignity, four words dependent on each other, and four words that sometimes seem like dreams too impossible to imagine. But it is important to remember that the answer to all five of our "will you" questions is, "I will, with God's help." We are followers, disciples on a path that has been set out and marked for us, and we can be confident that we are never alone in doing the work we have been given to do.

Early Christians called their movement The Way because they recognized that Jesus showed us a way to live. And this way is guided by love, not fear. It is guided by a theology of abundance, not scarcity. Following Christ's example, we must proclaim the Good News of God's love for all people. We are to embrace Jesus's message that God can always be found on the side of the marginalized and oppressed, on the side of justice. And we can look at the promises we make in our baptisms as a call always to be found there as well, participating in God's healing, reconciling, compassionate work in the world.

The arc of the moral universe does indeed bend toward
justice, but we are not called to sit by and watch it
bend. We are called as Christians to be jumping up and
down on it as Jesus did, helping it to bend, working to
make this church and this world more reflective of the
kingdom of God.

INVITATION

Think about the
contrast between
a theology of
abundance and a
theology of scarcity.
Which one better
describes your own
theology? What
fears hold you back
from peace and
justice work?

Will you strive for justice and peace among all people, and respect the dignity of every human being?

DAY TWO

Guiding scriptures for this week

Micah 6:6-8
"With what shall I come before the LORD, and bow myself before God on high? Shall I come before him with burnt offerings, with calves a year old? Will the LORD be pleased with thousands of rams, with ten thousands of rivers of oil? Shall I give my firstborn for my transgression, the fruit of my body for the sin of my soul?" He has told you, O mortal, what is good; and what does the LORD require of you but to do justice, and to love kindness, and to walk humbly with your God?

Matthew 25:34-40
Then the king will say to those at his right hand, "Come, you that are blessed by my Father, inherit the kingdom prepared for you from the foundation of the world; for I was hungry and you gave me food, I was thirsty and you gave me something to drink, I was a stranger and you welcomed me, I was naked and you gave me clothing, I was sick and you took care of me, I was in prison and you visited me." Then the righteous will answer him, "Lord, when was it that we saw you hungry and gave you food,

or thirsty and gave you something to drink? And when was it that we saw you a stranger and welcomed you, or naked and gave you clothing? And when was it that we saw you sick or in prison and visited you?" And the king will answer them, "Truly I tell you, just as you did it to one of the least of these who are members of my family, you did it to me."

John 4:34-38
Jesus said to them, "My food is to do the will of him who sent me and to complete his work. Do you not say, 'Four months more, then comes the harvest'? But I tell you, look around you, and see how the fields are ripe for harvesting. The reaper is already receiving wages and is gathering fruit for eternal life, so that sower and reaper may rejoice together. For here the saying holds true, 'One sows and another reaps.' I sent you to reap that for which you did not labor. Others have labored, and you have entered into their labor."

1 John 4:18-21
There is no fear in love, but perfect love casts out fear; for fear has to do with punishment, and whoever fears has not reached perfection in love. We love because he first loved us. Those who say, "I love God," and hate their brothers or sisters, are liars; for those who do not love a brother or sister whom they have seen, cannot love God whom they have not seen. The commandment we have from him is this: those who love God must love their brothers and sisters also.

INVITATION

As you prepare for the remainder of the week, consider what the Bible has to say about fulfilling this week's baptismal promise. Refer back to these verses throughout the week and make a note of additional scripture references that come to mind as you read.

DAY THREE

Will you strive for justice and peace among all people, and respect the dignity of every human being?

From Deuteronomy to the prophets to the words of Jesus in the gospels to Romans and Hebrews, scripture offers a clear biblical trajectory that advocates care for the stranger. The Jewish people were strangers in the land of Egypt and strangers in the Babylonian Empire during exile. Ruth, one of the great heroines of the Bible, moved to Bethlehem as a widowed and destitute stranger. The Holy Family themselves fled to Egypt as refugees and lived there until it was safe for them to return. And Jesus reiterated this focus on caring for the stranger throughout his ministry, saying that whatever is done for a stranger is done for him. Care for and identification with the stranger are central to who we are called to be as Christians.

St. Mark's Cathedral in Seattle, Washington, has answered this call by becoming part of the Sanctuary movement. In 2016, Jaime Rubio was facing deportation. St. Mark's invited him and his family to live on the cathedral grounds while he sought a legal remedy to allow him, his wife, and their young son to stay together. From 2016 to 2019, the Rubio family not only lived on church property but also became a vital part of the cathedral community.

The cathedral notes on its website, "In Christ's church, all are welcome, but it's not just in church—it is in our common life. St. Mark's stands in solidarity with all our neighbors, especially immigrants who are living in fear in these fraught times... Fundamental in the life of a Christian community, we take a stand to welcome the stranger, as our scriptures instruct."

St. Mark's and many other Episcopal congregations offer safe and welcoming spaces through their sanctuary ministries, serving as centers of community education for immigration issues and partnering with other secular and religious organizations to advocate for immigrant rights. These churches are living into the call of this week's baptismal promise, actively working for a more peaceful and just world for all.

INVITATION

Visit the website of Episcopal Migration Ministries at episcopalmigrationministries. org and click on "Resources" and "Resources for Congregations." Read about some of the ways that Episcopal churches can welcome and care for the stranger. How does, or could, your community follow this scriptural mandate in a way that makes sense in your local context?

To learn more about the Sanctuary ministry at St. Mark's Cathedral Seattle, visit saintmarks.org/justice/sanctuary.

DAY FOUR

*Will you strive for justice
and peace among all people,
and respect the dignity of
every human being?*

Put Forth, O God, Thy Spirit's Might

Put forth, O God, thy Spirit's might
and bid thy Church increase,
in breadth and length, in depth and height,
her unity and peace.

Let works of darkness disappear
before thy conquering light;
let hatred and tormenting fear
pass with the passing night.

Let what apostles learned of thee,
be ours from age to age;
their steadfast faith our unity,
their peace our heritage.

O Judge divine of human strife!
O Vanquisher of pain!
To know thee is eternal life,
to serve thee is to reign.

Lyrics by Howard Chandler Robbins,
The Hymnal 1982, 521

INVITATION

This hymn asks
God to put forth
the "Spirit's might
and bid the
Church increase,"
a clear reference
to evangelism. I
invite you to reflect
on different ways
this hymn can be interpreted using different
definitions of "evangelism."

*Will you strive for justice
and peace among all people,
and respect the dignity of
every human being?*

DAY FIVE

In April of 1963, eight clergymen from Alabama, two
of whom were the bishop and the bishop coadjutor
of the Episcopal Diocese of Alabama, wrote an open
letter urging the African American community to stop
participating in and supporting peaceful demonstrations
and acts of civil disobedience. They wanted the people of
Birmingham to be left alone to solve racial problems in
the city over time and according to local laws. They urged
negotiation through "proper" channels with local officials
and courts.

In his response, "Letter from Birmingham Jail," the Rev.
Dr. Martin Luther King, Jr. writes of his disappointment
in the "white moderate" who wants people to wait
patiently for rights that should have been theirs since
birth while trying to affect change through systems
designed to maintain the status quo. King writes that
"shallow understanding from people of goodwill is more
frustrating than absolute misunderstanding from people
of ill will." He lays out the difference between a positive
peace and a negative peace, with a negative peace being
"the absence of tension" and a positive peace as "the
presence of justice."

The Way of Jesus is a way of peace, but we cannot be satisfied with merely the absence of tension. A negative peace is only peaceful for those in power. It is not a true peace at all because it means that fairness and equity continue to be denied to those who have been silenced, to those who have already waited far too long for justice. We, as the church, must work toward a positive peace, a peace that applies to all of God's children.

INVITATION

I invite you to think about this contrast of negative and positive peace. Where do you see those currently in power advocating for a negative peace, and what response does our baptism call us to make? How does, or could, your church advocate for a positive peace in your community?

*Will you strive for justice
and peace among all people,
and respect the dignity of
every human being?*

DAY SIX

As human beings, we know something about fear. It is one of our most basic human emotions. And it can be constructive and healthy. It can keep us awake and aware of the world around us. It can urge us to seek shelter during a tornado and prevent us from stepping out in traffic without looking both ways. But it is easy to let fear cause us to abandon our responsibilities to God and to those around us. Fear can hinder us from proclaiming God's love. It can silence us in the face of injustice, and it can even motivate us to participate in the oppression of others.

Just as it can be scary to share our faith with others, it can be scary to stand up for the rights of others. But we can be confident, as Episcopalians, that we have a community of support around us. The Episcopal Church's Office of Social Justice and Advocacy Engagement works "to build community networks for justice by connecting and mobilizing people 'from the pews to the public square.'" Their website provides information on the church's partnership with the Poor People's Campaign, how individual parishes can partner with organizations like

RIP Medical Debt and the National Bail Fund Network, and resources for organizing public advocacy and faithful protesting ministries at the parish level.

The Episcopal Church's Office of Government Relations supports "legislation and policies that protect human rights, prevent atrocities, promote gender justice, and work toward reconciliation around the world." Information on the church's advocacy for the full inclusion of LGBTQ+ people in all aspects of society, its support for legislation to reduce gun violence, and its work to influence public policy to fight injustice in many other areas can be found on the government relations website.

We cannot let fear keep us from working toward God's vision for the world, that all people be reconciled to God and each other. In her book *The Dream of God: A Call to Return,* the noted lay leader Verna Dozier wrote, "Doubt is not the opposite of faith. Fear is. Fear will not risk that even if I am wrong, I will trust that if I move today by the light that is given me, knowing it is only finite and partial, I will know more and different things tomorrow than I know today, and I can be open to the new possibility I cannot even imagine today."

INVITATION

What do you see as an individual Christian's role in politics and public policy? What do you see as the church's role? I invite you to spend time exploring the Episcopal Church's websites, especially those focused on social justice and government relations. Reflect on whether God is calling you to join these ministries.

Visit these sites: episcopalchurch.org/ministries/ social-justice-advocacy-engagement

episcopalchurch.org/ministries/office-government-relations

DAY SEVEN

Will you strive for justice and peace among all people, and respect the dignity of every human being?

Post-communion Prayer
The Book of Common Prayer, p.366

Almighty and everliving God,
we thank you for feeding us with the spiritual food
of the most precious Body and Blood
of your Son our Savior Jesus Christ;
and for assuring us in these holy mysteries
that we are living members of the Body of your Son,
and heirs of your eternal kingdom.
And now, Father, send us out
to do the work you have given us to do,
to love and serve you
as faithful witnesses of Christ our Lord.
To him, to you, and to the Holy Spirit,
be honor and glory, now and
for ever. *Amen.*

Afterword

The Gospel of John records: "It is finished" (John 19:30). It is finished. In Jesus Christ, the communication of God's love for all people is complete. Jesus has shown us how to lay down our lives for each other, both in our living and in our dying. The Way of Love is open.

In our Baptismal Covenant, we have promised to follow Jesus along this way of love, to step outside of our church doors and to participate in God's healing, compassionate, reconciling work in the world. As we have explored these "will you" questions and what they have to say about evangelism, I hope you have been inspired to take part in this work in new ways in your own context. All the resources referenced throughout this study—organizations, books, and websites—are compiled in the appendix for easy reference. I encourage you to use them and further explore how you and your faith community can follow the call to discipleship and evangelism.

Remember that the answer to this call is, "I will, with God's help." Jesus promised in John 14:26, "But the Advocate, the Holy Spirit, whom the Father will send in my name, will teach you everything, and remind you of all that I have said to you." God is with us every step along this way as our guide, comforter, advocate, and companion. We are not alone.

As we prepare for Good Friday, the Great Vigil, and
Easter Sunday, I want to thank you for taking this
Lenten journey with me. We discussed in Week One
how the post-communion prayer is a commissioning
for evangelism that we pray for ourselves and each other
every week in the eucharistic service. I invite you to
incorporate that prayer into your daily life, letting its
words inspire and encourage you to the work God has
given you so that you might love and serve as faithful
witnesses of Christ our Lord.

Amen.

Resources

WEEK ONE

This Band of Sisterhood: Black Women Bishops edited by Westina Matthews

Centering Prayer and Inner Awakening by Cynthia Bourgeault

The Center for Spiritual Imagination, ministry of Cathedral of the Incarnation, Garden City, New York
    www.spiritualimagination.org

The Contemplative Society, contemplative.org

WEEK TWO

All Shall Be Well: A Modern-Language Version of the Revelation of Julian of Norwich by Ellyn Sanna

Indigenous Ministries, ministry of the Episcopal Church
    episcopalchurch.org/ministries/indigenous-
    ministries/

Tell Me the Truth about Racism, curriculum by Jen Holt Enriquez and Will Bouvel
    tellmethetruthaboutracism.org

Sacred Ground: A Race Dialogue Series, curriculum of the Episcopal Church
    episcopalchurch.org/sacred-ground

WEEK THREE

Evangelism Ministries, ministry of the Episcopal Church
  episcopalchurch.org/ministries/evangelism/

Walking on Water: Reflections on Faith and Art by
Madeleine L'Engle

Evangelism Charter for the Episcopal Church
  episcopalchurch.org/ministries/evangelism/toolkit/
  foundations/

History and Reconciliation Initiative, ministry of
St. Paul's Episcopal Church, Richmond, Virginia
  stpaulsrva.org/HRI

WEEK FOUR

Tattoos on the Heart: The Power of Boundless Compassion
by Greg Boyle

Founders Place, ministry of St. Luke's Episcopal Church,
Birmingham, Alabama
  saint-lukes.com/ministries/founders-place/

Stand Your Ground: Black Bodies and the Justice of God
by Kelly Brown Douglas

WEEK FIVE

Sanctuary at St. Mark's, ministry of St. Mark's Episcopal Cathedral, Seattle, Washington
saintmarks.org/justice/sanctuary

Episcopal Migration Ministries, ministry of the Episcopal Church
episcopalmigrationministries.org

"Letter from Birmingham Jail" by Martin Luther King Jr.

Social Justice and Advocacy Engagement, ministry of the Episcopal Church
episcopalchurch.org/ministries/social-justice-advocacy-engagement

Government Relations, ministry of the Episcopal Church
episcopalchurch.org/ministries/office-government-relations/

The Dream of God: A Call to Return by Verna Dozier

Acknowledgments

Thank you to my husband Wil and our son Darwin, who have been so patient, kind, encouraging, and consistently and embarrassingly proud throughout this long process. I love you both so much.

To the Rt. Rev. Phoebe A. Roaf, the Rev. Canon Sharon Alexander, the Rev. Dr. Dorothy Sanders Wells, Day Smith-Pritchartt and the board and staff of the Episcopal Evangelism Society, and Richelle Thompson and the entire team at Forward Movement, thank you for your unfailing support, wisdom, and guidance.

A special note of thanks to Lee Nix, who facilitated the first pilot group of this curriculum, and to the good people at Church of the Good Shepherd in Memphis, Tennessee, who tested the initial draft with her, including the Rev. Dr. Noah Campbell, Suzy Askew, Cheryl Morgan Barton, Bobbi Dodge, John Lynch, Patrick Lynch, Shari Moore, Larry Rains, Sherry Sachritz, Bill Scarborough, Pam Scarborough, and John P. Vergos.

Thank you to all of those who participated in and facilitated pilot groups at Church of the Holy Apostles, Collierville, Tennessee; St. Christopher's Church, Oak Park, Illinois; Christ Church, Kensington, Maryland;

Church of the Advocate, Chapel Hill, North Carolina; St. Mark's Church, Clifford, Virginia; Grace Church, Massies Mill, Virginia; Church of the Good Shepherd, Federal Way, Washington; St. Paul's Church, Chattanooga, Tennessee; and St. Phillip's Church, Hearne, Texas. This was truly a group effort, and your feedback and insight were invaluable.

About the Author

Amanda Perkins McGriff lives in Memphis, Tennessee, with her husband of twenty years, Wil, their son Darwin, and their retired greyhound Goose. She is an Episcopal priest and currently serves as a chaplain at Le Bonheur Children's Hospital, ministering to children, families, and staff in the neonatal intensive care unit and the emergency department.

After graduation from Bexley Seabury Seminary in Chicago, she received a 2021 Episcopal Evangelism Society grant that led to the creation of *Will You? A Lenten Study of Baptismal Promises*, a curriculum exploring connections between baptism, eucharist, and evangelism. Her vocation as a priest, her work as a hospital chaplain, and her call as a follower of Christ form the foundation for this book and for her ministry.

About Forward Movement

Forward Movement inspires disciples and empowers evangelists. People around the world read daily devotions through *Forward Day by Day*, which is also available in Spanish (*Adelante Día a Día*) and Braille, online, as a podcast, and as an app for smartphones.

We actively seek partners across the church and look for ways to provide resources that inspire and challenge. A ministry of the Episcopal Church since 1935, Forward Movement is a nonprofit organization funded by sales of resources and gifts from generous donors.

To learn more about Forward Movement and our work, visit us at ForwardMovement.org or VenAdelante.org. We are delighted to be doing this work and invite your prayers and support.